pilgrims of hope

The People Of The Catholic Diocese Of Cleveland

And Bishop Anthony M. Pilla Reflect On 25 Years Together.

All proceeds from the sale of this book go to

The Bishop Pilla Legacy of Hope Jubilee Foundation

for the education and training of those who teach

the Catholic faith and for tuition assistance

for the children of Catholic School teachers.

Brothers and sisters:
Let love be sincere;
hate what is evil,
hold on to what is good;
love one another with mutual affection;
anticipate one another in showing honor.
Do not grow slack in zeal,
be fervent in spirit,
serve the Lord.
Rejoice in hope,
endure in affliction,
persevere in prayer.
Contribute to the needs of the holy ones,
exercise hospitality.
Bless those who persecute you,
bless and do not curse them.
Rejoice with those who rejoice,
weep with those who weep.
Have the same regard for one another;
do not be haughty but associate with the lowly;
do not be wise in your own estimation.

Romans 12:9-16

MANETE IN DILECTIONE MEA

When I preside at the Eucharist, especially before large assemblies such

as today, I am deeply moved as I see you gathered with me in prayer.

I see faces young, old, middle-aged, black, white, yellow, red and brown,

and read in them the histories of struggle and pain mixed with joy and

hope. In my mind's eye, I picture those forebears in faith who came here

from Europe, Africa, Asia and Latin America. When I look at you, who

are both my flock and my brothers and sisters, I am often deeply moved,

because I love you very much and, uniting myself with Jesus,

the Good Shepherd, I am ready to lay down my life for you.

Jubilee Year Homily, Public Auditorium
Bishop Anthony M. Pilla
January 7, 2001

contents

A Letter from The Most Reverend Anthony M. Pilla,
Bishop of Cleveland

foreword

Pilgrims of Hope! On January 6, 1981, Bishop Anthony M. Pilla was installed as the ninth Bishop of the Diocese of Cleveland. On that day, after introducing himself as "Anthony, your brother," Bishop Pilla invited the people of Cleveland to join him on a pilgrimage of hope. No one could have imagined where that journey would take us – but we were assured that, from that first step, God's gift of hope would be our guide, our guard and our destination.

January 6, 2006, marks the 25th anniversary of Bishop Pilla's installation. He is the longest-serving bishop in the 158-year history of the Diocese of Cleveland. While this jubilee is clearly a milestone in the Bishop's life, it also marks the passage of a significant period in the life of the people of the Diocese of Cleveland. We have created this edition as both a commemoration of Bishop Pilla's anniversary and a reflection upon this quarter century in our Church's history.

At the dawn of the Third Millennium, the Diocese of Cleveland claims more than 800,000 members in a metropolitan area of over three million people. A rich ethnic diversity, old city neighborhoods and long-standing parish pride are among the great qualities of this diocesan family. Bishop Pilla is the first native-born son – the first priest of this Diocese – to serve as its Catholic leader. His faith and priesthood were born of those traditions. The Bishop's Italian-American family, his beloved diocesan priesthood in Jesus Christ, and his cherished city of Cleveland are all manifest in an unflinching pastoral love of and dedication to the "good people" he has now served for a quarter century.

The Church of the Diocese of Cleveland has earned a national reputation as a steadfast, yet innovative, leader. Our Catholic Charities Health and Human Services system, excellent Catholic Schools, proactive social ministries and beautiful liturgies are renowned. The fact that so many individuals and ministries from our local Church have flourished and gained acclaim is a tribute to Bishop Pilla's strength as a leader and his personal humility as a shepherd. His distinction as a pastor was acknowledged even by his peers when, in 1996, Bishop Pilla was the first Bishop of Cleveland to ever be elected as president of the United States Conference of Catholic Bishops.

The vision and faith of Bishop Pilla are reflected and can be seen in the life of the Church he leads. Conversely, the Church of the Diocese of Cleveland is visible and can be seen in the convictions, ministries and words of this bishop who came forth from us. We share a common origin, a core set of values, a unity of spirit and a faith that is uniquely our own.

Among the core values that have guided the Church over these two decades is Bishop Pilla's conviction that every child deserves a quality education. Next to life and faith, a quality education is the greatest gift we can offer our young people. To educate a child is an act of hope. To that end, The Bishop Pilla Legacy of Hope Jubilee Foundation has been established to ensure that this commitment lives on into the future. The proceeds from this book will supply initial funding for this foundation, which will provide for the education and training of those who teach the Catholic faith and tuition assistance for the children of Catholic School teachers.

As Bishop Pilla approaches his 75th birthday on November 12, 2007, we anticipate the conclusion of his service as our shepherd. But the pilgrimage of hope, to which he calls us, will not end. As the Bishop retires, this book is intended to be a cherished memoir of this important period in our diocesan history. It is with gratitude to God for all that has been accomplished in our midst over these 25 years that we set forth the following words, images and memories. For the Church and the Bishop, may these photographs and messages help us to remember our story and reflect upon the meaning of our journey. As pilgrims stepping onto the next leg of the journey, may the prayerful remembrance of our story console us, encourage us and give us hope.

Legacy Book Project Committee

introduction

"Come with me."

"The Magi, whose fabled journey to Christ has long been celebrated on this twelfth day of Christmas, were on a great pilgrimage of faith, hope and love; a pilgrimage to Christ, guided by the bright light of the morning star. On this day I begin a new pilgrimage. And I want each of you to come with me. Come with me on a Pilgrimage of Hope! Come with me on a pilgrimage to Christ!"

With these words at his installation as the ninth Bishop of the Catholic Diocese of Cleveland on January 6, 1981, Bishop Anthony M. Pilla called the faithful to join him on a glorious journey – a Pilgrimage of Hope. Today, more than twenty-five years along this road, those pilgrims of hope pause here, in these pages, to celebrate and to reflect upon a quarter century of sadness and joy, difficulty and determination, setbacks and success. With each step on this journey – with the guidance and companionship of "their Bishop" – the good people of this Diocese have been gathered in love, strengthened by prayer, sustained by faith and encouraged by hope.

The message and the leadership of Bishop Pilla during this quarter of a century have called and formed the community of believers and the people of this region to seek a new vision of hope. That vision has taken shape in six discernible characteristics of the Church itself, touchstones by which the progress of the Church and the community at large can be measured: Community, Faith, Responsibility, Justice, Compassion and Hope. Under each of these headings, page by page, in the following chapters, one can hear the echoes of Bishop Pilla's words; words that inspire and reassure. In the photographs, gathered from these many years on the journey, the reader may now revisit scenes and faces that have illuminated and blessed the path.

How far we, the Pilgrim Church, have journeyed! And how rich are the opportunities on the road ahead. We rejoice in the blessings of the past and embrace the promise and hope of all that is yet to be. "Come with me."

At the Installation Liturgy on January 6, 1981, Bishop Pilla preaches his first homily as the Catholic leader
of the Church he loves, calling all of us to a "pilgrimage of hope."

Bishop Pilla was ordained a priest in 1959 and, 22 years later at the age of 48, was the first priest of the Diocese of Cleveland ever to be installed as its bishop. The Bishop's 25th Anniversary of Priesthood Ordination was celebrated with special solemnity and joy in 1984.

community

The Family Bond.

"We do not make that journey alone. We make it together."

Drawing us together for solace and strength, reaching out to create solidarity – community is the bond that forges us into a unity of purpose. Bishop Pilla's earliest life experiences in a simple Italian-American family became the model for his role among all those he cares about. This motif of welcoming and supportive family is overriding and pervasive in his thoughts, words and ministry. He builds family bonds.

So it is with the people of the Diocese of Cleveland. This family is not just a statement of relationship – it is ethnic, emotional, celebrated, feasted upon, sung about. "When you're in trouble," Bishop Pilla says, "it's your family that comes around." And for the Bishop that family includes the unexpected and previously unimagined. His is a call to community that transcends the boundaries of Church, race, politics and religion. It now includes ecumenical and interfaith partners, civic, business and political leaders, parents who long for quality education for their children, new immigrants, cherished ethnic neighborhoods and so many more. It embraces all people who desire to walk the journey of hope. This family of hope now understands what the Bishop meant at his installation when he said, "I am Anthony, your brother."

Within this family of communal life an invitation rings, "Come in. You're welcome. You're home." A place at the table is not merely a nice phrase. It is the strategy the Bishop has put to work in all of his ministry. "Get everyone at the table who ought to be there. Make room at the table for anyone who wants to be there."

We're all there. As a Church and as one People of God, we have been called by this brother-become-bishop to extend that family design into all that we do.

Family and community were nurtured in the Bishop's heart at home with his mother and father, Libera and George Pilla, and his only sibling, Joseph. Bishop Pilla greets his family at the liturgy celebrating the conclusion of the Jubilee Year and the Bishop's 20th anniversary of installation on January 6, 2001, at Cleveland's Public Hall.

Dressed in traditional clothing, these two girls represented one of the 63 ethnic groups in the Diocese at the Sesquicentennial Celebration on August 17, 1997, at Cleveland's Public Hall.

"*The reason we come back here each year is because we love our 'mother.' This church, this neighborhood, these values and traditions – they are our mother. And you know, as with the Lord Himself, we respect and care for our mother. We need to remember that, and we need to pass that on to our children. The values, the dignity, the respect and tradition that we have learned here is what the next generation needs in order to live a good and fulfilling life with God and neighbor.*"

Annual Solemnity of the Assumption of Mary
Holy Rosary Church in Cleveland's Little Italy

"*The Church of the Home is a miniature faith community because in this small domestic church, family members can experience the Kingdom of God. We will change the world if we believe that our values have meaning.*"

"The Christian Family: The Church of the Home"
Pastoral Letter on the Family
September 21, 1986

The largest of its kind in the United States, Cleveland's "Little Italy" neighborhood on Mayfield Road hosts the region's most celebrated ethnic festival. The Bishop celebrates 'The Feast' of the Assumption of Mary with Mass and procession every August 15th on 'the Hill' at Holy Rosary Church where he was baptized in 1932.

The embrace of God's love extends to all people. Bishop Pilla celebrates with neighborhood children in the 2000 dedication ceremony of the Fatima Family Center, 6600 Lexington Avenue, just one of 62 Catholic Charities locations providing 176 different programs throughout the Diocese.

*"**As important as one's particular gifts, as great as anyone's individual talent may be, none of us, by ourselves, can make up the Church, the people that God has called from darkness into His marvelous light."*

USCCB Presidential Address
Washington, D.C.
November 16, 1998

The 2001 Liturgy for the Certification of Lay Ecclesial Ministers at the Cathedral of St. John the Evangelist. Since 1985, over 290 theologically and pastorally trained lay women and men have been certified by the Diocese to serve as leaders and collaborators in the pastoral ministry of the Church.

"I issued a statement which expressed a challenge to build new cities – cities where people of different incomes, races and cultures can live together and be enriched together. Neighborhoods with mixed incomes, cultures and religions enrich everyone. They become a witness of how we are meant to live together."

"To Serve the Common Good."
National Preservation Conference, Cleveland, Ohio
October 2002

Christian ecumenical leaders representing the rich traditions of faith in our region anticipate the entrance procession of the diocesan sesquicentennial celebration in 1997 at Public Hall.

"I do not wish to leave you with the impression that all the challenges to Jewish-Christian reconciliation have been met 'in our time.' They have not. Anti-Semitism remains a serious problem which Jews and Christians must face together. But a very real beginning has been made. And the future opens up infinite possibilities for joint witness and action for 'mending the world' so needed today."

Park Synagogue
April 7, 1995

A unique and unprecedented relationship between Christians and Jews is expressed in the Diocese of Cleveland through mutual respect, formal initiatives and personal friendships. Bishop Pilla and Rabbi Howard Ruben participate in a special 2000 Holocaust Memorial at the Fairmount Temple in Beachwood, Ohio.

"*When life is difficult or sad, it is your family that gathers around you. That is the case for us today as a Church and you – our family and friends – it is good that you have gathered with us to pray.*"

Comments to Interfaith and Ecumenical Leaders
Vespers Upon the Death of the Pope
Cathedral of Saint John the Evangelist
April 4, 2005

The order of bishops, or the college as they are called, form a community of leadership and a fraternity of brothers. Bishop Pilla greets Auxiliary Bishops Pevec and Gries, as well as the Eparch, Bishop Basil Schott, of the Byzantine Eparchy of Parma – Ruthenian Rite – (now the Metropolitan Archbishop of the Byzantine Archeparchy of Pittsburgh) at the 20th anniversary of Bishop Pilla's Installation, January 6, 2001.

"So often we talk in terms of the 'needs' of the older people and we forget about the talent of the older people. Whenever we talk of older people, so often, we talk about what we need to do for them, forgetting that they can do a lot for us."

Dedication of new Nativity Manor
Nativity of Blessed Virgin Mary Parish, Lorain, Ohio
December 13, 2004

In addition to celebrating annual Senior Day with Masses throughout the Diocese, the cherished elderly of the Diocese are an important and faithful segment of the People of God. This blessing of Saint Patrick Manor in Wellington, Ohio in 1999 is an expression of the way we care for our seniors.

"Whhen I look at the challenges facing us on our journey into the future, I am certain that we must commit ourselves to making this notion of togetherness, or collaboration, the foundation of our mission and the basis of our hope."

Jubilee Year Mass Homily
Cleveland Public Hall
January 7, 2001

The Hispanic Ministry of our Diocese, the fastest growing ethnic ministry, is beautifully expressed in the 1996 merger of Cleveland's Capilla del Cristo Rey and San Juan Bautista parishes to form a new parish, La Sagrada Familia, and by the 1997 construction of the first Catholic church built in the city of Cleveland since St. Agnes/Our Lady of Fatima church in 1983.

For several years the Asian Ministry has formed to incorporate and celebrate some of our newest immigrants including Filipino, Vietnamese, Japanese, Chinese, Asian, Indian, Korean and Indonesian. This incense rite is a feature of the Annual Asian Mass.

"This is an awesome day, a day of countless blessings, and not just those of a diocese celebrating 150 years. This is a day of countless blessings of all the children of God, everywhere, this is the day the Lord has made, this is a day of victory for our God."

Diocesan Sesquicentennial Mass Homily
Cleveland Public Hall
August 17, 1997

The restoration of the Diaconate has produced 198 deacons for service in our Diocese who, together with their wives and children, have enriched the ministry of the Word, Sacrament and Charity.

Opposite: Young and old attend the 'Fest' on the grounds of the Center for Pastoral Leadership in Wickliffe. This event has drawn thousands of young people and families for fun, music and prayer every August since 2000.

The United States Conference of Catholic Bishops is an experience of community and collaboration for our nation's bishops as they lead the Catholic Church in our country. In addition to delivering the Presidential Address annually from 1995-1998, Bishop Pilla enjoyed the fraternity of his brother bishops as pictured here with Bishop Lynch of St. Petersburg, Florida and Bishop Doran of Rockford, Illinois.

"Your faith and zeal for the Church have been a source of support for my own vocation. I thank God for those of you with whom I have worked personally. And I am grateful for the vision of the Council without which I may not have had the opportunity to do so."

NCCB Presidential Address, Comment to Religious
Washington, D.C.
November 16, 1998

63 different religious communities of women and men consisting of 1,425 persons are currently serving in our Diocese. The contributions of these sisters, brothers and priests to our mission and institutions is incalculable. The new life and changing reality of religious is expressed in this 2004 merger of our diocesan Vincentian Sisters of Charity (founded 1929) with the Sisters of Charity of Cincinnati.

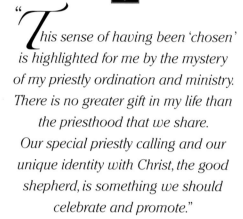

"*This sense of having been 'chosen' is highlighted for me by the mystery of my priestly ordination and ministry. There is no greater gift in my life than the priesthood that we share. Our special priestly calling and our unique identity with Christ, the good shepherd, is something we should celebrate and promote.*"

Lenten Letter to Priests
March 2001

"*No one is too poor to contribute; no one too rich to benefit. The emphasis is on what we can accomplish together for the common good...if we know each other, and especially if we are friends. If we are friends, a great deal is possible.*"

National Symposium on The Church in the City
Keynote Address
The Temple-Tifereth Israel
April 20, 1998

Beginning with the ordination in 1981 as pictured here, Bishop Pilla has ordained 146 diocesan priests for service in our 234 parishes. St. Mary Seminary is one of the largest of its kind in the country preparing men for ordination to the priesthood and diaconate and others seeking theological training. They offer the Master of Divinity, Master of Arts in Theology and the Doctor of Ministry degrees.

"*We not only have a place in the Body of Christ, the Church, but all of us share in the mission of building up the Church and witnessing to God's Reign in our joys, struggles and journey of life. I have established the Gay and Lesbian Family Ministry to provide pastoral care for our homosexual brothers and sisters and their families in fidelity to the teachings of the Church. It is my hope that this ministry can be an opportunity for healing and reconciliation.*"

Diocesan Brochure
Gay and Lesbian Family Ministry
1998

"*Whether people belong to an urban, suburban, exurban or rural parish, we are all called to be one body with one mission. In the context of our faith, this call to unity is not an option. It is who we are as a Catholic Church. We are called to be a single faith community, respecting our diversity but united in solidarity with the whole human family.*"

City Club Address
June 14, 1996

Our diversity as a community of faith is most visible when we celebrate. These Lithuanian dancers from Our Lady of Perpetual Help parish on Cleveland's East Side entertain at the 1984 Silver Jubilee of Bishop Pilla's priesthood ordination.

Multi-cultural events are important to the life of our Diocese in which we blend the older European and the new Latino, Asian and African traditions which include music, traditional garb, prayer and food.

克城華寄

faith

A God-Centered Life.

"Ask yourself, what does God want me to do with my life?"

A community of believers is born, rooted in, and empowered by faith. Faith comforts us, gives us strength, and makes us steadfast to do the work it requires. Faith in a loving God is the heart of the Church community and the individual believer; certainly it is the heart of Bishop Pilla. He prays for the Church and the world always. Growing in that faith – and building a community that reflects the love of God – is our tradition.

Fidelity is an attribute of faith. Being faithful to what the Church teaches, how the Church celebrates, what the Church proclaims, who the Church is – are all aspects of diocesan life under Bishop Pilla's leadership. This, the Catholic faith of our Diocese, is expressed in a passionate, lively and very diverse community of believers throughout our eight counties. Bishop Pilla is known for respecting the unique, local qualities of that faith. And that respect is one of the things for which he is loved and appreciated. This tapestry of ethnic, urban, rural and suburban faith is both simple in its love of God and complex in its many forms and faces. It gives birth to possibility and hope.

And while the possibilities sometimes overwhelm our imaginations, we nonetheless endeavor to honor all that the Catholic Church embraces. It's what

Bishop Pilla has called us to do – creating unity in the midst of diversity. Whether it is the Eucharist, the Mother of God, the sanctity of life, the call to holiness of all the Christian faithful, the importance of marriage, a preferential care for the poor, an evangelization that welcomes, dignity for vocations to all Church ministries, sound theological and continuing formation, good and inclusive liturgy, quality Catholic education, sincere collaboration or healthy diversity – we work to do all that is respectful of our tradition. We strive to be Catholic to the fullest – with zeal, joy and creativity.

This faith and its multi-faceted expressions are what we love about being Catholics from the Diocese of Cleveland. In the words of a former Cleveland priest, now retired bishop of another Diocese, *"No one does Church like Cleveland!"*

To Bishop Pilla, the Eucharist is the daily source of our faith lives. The Eucharist is the goal of all that we believe and hope for as Catholics – it makes us one. The Bishop celebrates Mass on his 20th anniversary of installation as Bishop of the Diocese in 2001.

Pope John Paul II and Bishop Pilla at their last personal meeting in Rome on May 6, 2004.
Pope John Paul called Bishop Pilla to the episcopacy and saluted the Bishop on his 25 years in office
just months before the Pontiff's death in 2005.

"*H*is personal holiness radiates from him as a personal communication from God. It resonated in his voice, it enlivened his eyes, and it penetrated anyone who was with him."

Mass upon the Death of Pope John Paul II Homily
Cathedral of Saint John the Evangelist
April 5, 2005

"*G*od sees things quite differently than we do. He sees deep beneath the surface appearances of life. He sees into the very heart of things. Whether a person is well dressed or poorly attired, whether a person is highly educated or never finished grade school, whether a person celebrates Christmas in a mansion or in a prison – none of that, in itself, is important or impressive in God's eyes."

Jubilee Year Christmas Message
Catholic Universe Bulletin
December 2000

"$\mathcal{B}$y Baptism, we are called to serve each other. None of us needs a distinct mandate to carry out that commission. It comes to us from the Lord. It is unmistakably His commission to every baptized person. I can never dispense you or myself from doing what the Lord commands us."

Federation of Catholic Community Services Annual Meeting
May 14, 1981

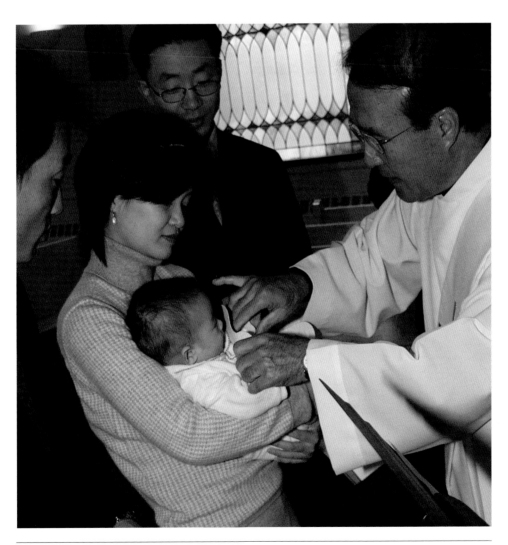

Baptism incorporates each individual into the community of the faithful and is the source of faith and eternal life. An infant is baptized at Saint Andrew Kim Pastoral Center, the spiritual home of 210 Korean families from around the Diocese, established in 1988.

"So, although we come to dedicate this great 'temple' as a new home for the worshipping Church, every indication is that the Holy Spirit wants to rededicate each of us as living stones in the City of God. What we do today looks as if it's about a building, but what it's really about is believing."

Dedication of a Church Homily
St. Edward Church, Ashland, Ohio
December 17, 2000

Bishop Pilla has celebrated the formal Rite of Dedication for most of the new parish churches built in the past 25 years during which he anoints the walls and the altar with the oil of Sacred Chrism as he did at Saint John Vianney Parish, Mentor, Ohio on September 29, 2002.

"If we are not a people of prayer, we will wither. Prayer is the fountain that overflows into all else we do. Prayer is the oasis that restores our parched spirits when we must cross deserts of despair. Prayer is the water, the fire of the Holy Spirit that gathers us together in a new Pentecost."

Mass of Installation Homily
Cathedral of Saint John the Evangelist
January 6, 1981

"This is a great parish. This is a great parish not because of its beautiful architecture, its wonderful organizations and ministries, or the effective programming you offer. Parishes like this one are great parishes because people find themselves loved here. This is a great parish – because it is a community of great love."

Anniversary of the Laying of the Cornerstone Homily
St. Bernard Church, Akron, Ohio
June 23, 2002

Our obligation and privilege as members of the Church is to pass on our faith, especially to the children. Teaching and celebrating the faith with and for the young is a primary call and ministry within our local Church.

"*It has been the experience of many of us that 'where mother is – there is the heart, the home and the essence of family.' The same can be said of our family of faith, the Church. Devotion to the Mother of God has been with the Church in every place and time and within every culture of the world. Artistic renderings and popular piety inspired by Mary reveal the deepest concerns, hopes and aspirations of people everywhere.*"

Letter to the Diocese
"The Many Faces of Mary" Art Exhibit
October 4, 2001

Our celebration of the Third Christian Millennium included an acknowledgment of the multi-cultural nature of the Church in the United States. This tapestry of cultures and our love for Mary, the Mother of God, was expressed in a 2001 art show entitled "The Many Faces of Mary." Bishop Pilla's contribution to that exhibit is pictured above, on the right.

*"My mother was clearly the presider in our household of faith.
She was a veritable powerhouse of prayer and a model of trust in the Lord."*

Funeral Mass Homily for Bishop Pilla's Mother, Libera Pilla
Cathedral of Saint John the Evangelist
February 1, 2003

Family love and support is prominent in the ministry of our Diocese and in the preaching of Bishop Pilla,
a message inspired by the faith and devotion of his parents. Mrs. Pilla prays at the Bishop's installation in
1981 in the Cathedral of St. John the Evangelist.

"Our journey into a new century and millennium will find women continuing to say 'yes' in new and different ways. Not only will they continue to change and shape the face of our society and culture, but they will also bring a new spirit and their own unique gifts to the church and to church leadership. Women are a vibrant and vital presence in the church."

Let's Celebrate Women's Vibrant Presence
"Live on In My Love", Catholic Universe Bulletin
March 17, 2000

"The starting point of discerning what God is saying to us today is to ask what is God doing in the midst of this people this day."

"Let Your Word Rain Down"
Pastoral Letter on the Ministry of the Word
1995

"Just as this fantastic structure was built according to an architect's design with crisp lines, impressive arches, brilliant light, and stone of every kind – so have our lives been scripted to the plan of God's Holy Word and redeemed in the pattern of His Son, Jesus Christ."

Dedication of a Church Homily
Saint Joseph Church, Avon Lake, Ohio
June 25, 2000

The primary role of the presbyter is to proclaim the Good News to all people and Bishop Pilla has been an effective and consistent communicator of the faith in many places – most prominently in the pulpit (ambo) of our Cathedral of St. John the Evangelist as pictured here.

*"M*y hope is that we will do
all that is possible to sustain and
enhance the vibrant parish life to
which Jesus calls us – for every
parishioner and for our priests and
parish ministers. If the Church is to
flourish in the 21st century, we must
offer, maintain and support a vibrant
parish life for every Catholic."

"Vibrant Parish Life"
Pastoral Letter on Parish Life
February 2001

Hundreds of Catechumens and Candidates for
Easter Sacraments (over 1,200 in 2005) gather with the
Bishop at Public Hall for the Rite of Election every Lent.
These converts, adults and children, are initiated as
a sign of faith and new life in the Church.

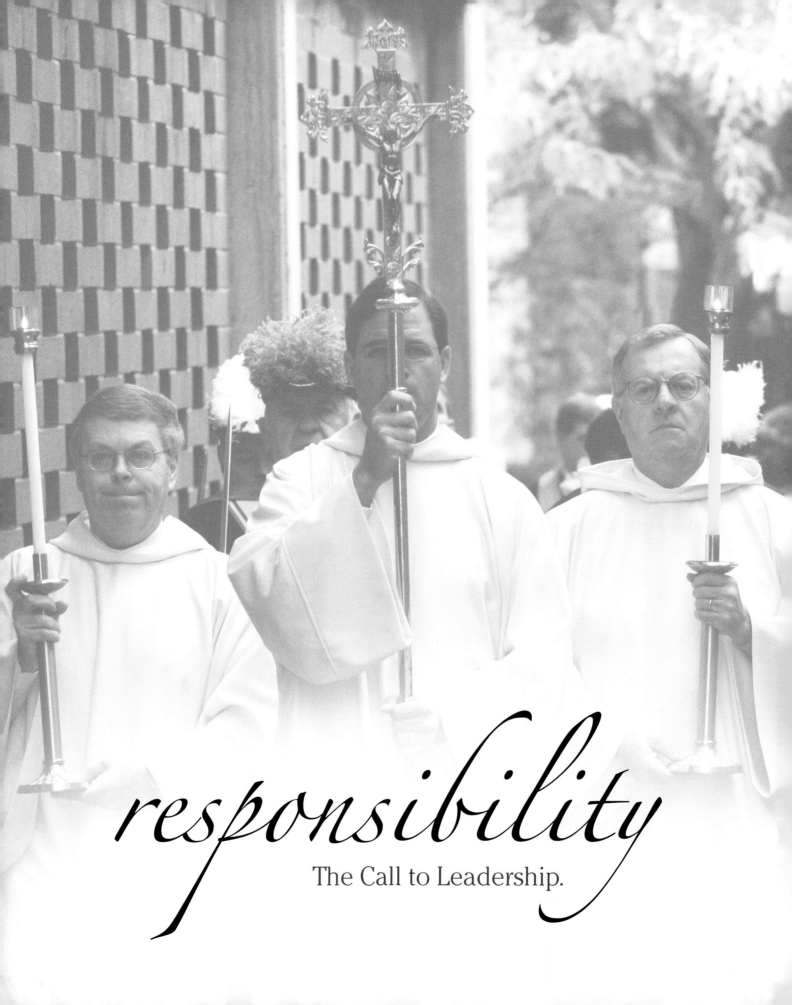

responsibility

The Call to Leadership.

"Not because they are poor and oppressed, overlooked, persecuted… not because they are Catholic, but because we are."

Faith points us towards responsibility, the commitment to lead. Leadership is hard to define, easy to recognize. We know it when we see it. To lead is a quality we find in Jesus and a gift of the Spirit. To discern where to step when everyone is frozen in fear, shame, denial or rage – that is leadership. Bishop Pilla has shown us what faithful responsibility is, and he has called us to take the responsibility that our faith demands. He insists that we face up to the tough issues in our civic life, unpopular initiatives of peace and the economy, the environment and more. In fact, if it weren't for the tough issues, we wouldn't need great leaders. Following Bishop Pilla, who leads with steadfast determination in the face of insult or applause, we have become a more responsible Church – leaders in faith.

Responsibility in faith draws us into dialogue with the world around us. As Americans of every stripe we share daily in a wonderful and sometimes challenging plurality. For some, our tradition of "Separation of Church and State" has been interpreted to mean that faith ought to be excluded from society and public life. Not so for our Bishop. Quietly, but clearly, the Bishop has challenged all the people of our region to allow our faith in God, our values and virtues, to impact our lives in the world.

The Gospel cannot thrive if it is left to Sunday morning. It was never intended to be thus. Being responsible with our faith leads us into respectful debate, cooperative enterprises, and public stances every day of the week. That is our Catholic Tradition, it is the conviction of our Bishop, and it has become the hallmark of our Church in the Diocese of Cleveland. We stand for something. That is our faith.

Celebrations of joy and gratitude can also further the mission of the church as in the 1997 diocesan sesquicentennial walk-a-thon/pray-a-thon in which these religious men and women celebrated by raising awareness and money to fund Church in the City initiatives and housing needs of the poor.

"I personally am deeply grateful for the opportunity to improve our community, and I believe that our problems can be overcome. With unshakable faith, I believe that we can awaken the people in our community to action and that people of goodwill working together can achieve a community which is strong and caring for all."

"Common Ground for the Common Good"
Proceedings from The Church in the City Regional Forums
1998-1999

Along with our growing elderly population is the increasing need for adequate housing so that our seniors can remain in their life-long neighborhoods and parishes. Catholic Charities and local parishes have taken the lead in developing over 1,000 senior housing units throughout the region such as this one at Annunciation Parish in Akron, Ohio.

While leading the United States Conference of Catholic Bishops, Bishop Pilla presided over the landmark statements "The Challenge of Peace" and "Economic Justice for All." Here he accepts congratulations from Cardinal Joseph Bernardin of Chicago on his 1995 election as USCCB President.

"$\mathcal{D}$*efending the human dignity of the poor and their hope for a human future is not a luxury for the church, nor is it a strategy for opportunism, nor a means for currying favor with the masses. It is her duty because it is God who wishes all human beings to live in accordance with the dignity that He bestowed on them."*

"A Call to Care for One Another"
Pastoral Letter
October 4, 1981

While Bishop Pilla most enjoys ministry when among the people of the Diocese, the majority of his daily work takes place in his office on Cathedral Square in the Chancery Building. He shares this pastoral responsibility with many diocesan staff members, but most personally with Miss Eileen VonAlt, secretary to the Bishop since 1975 when "Fr. Pilla" was Secretary for Clergy and Religious.

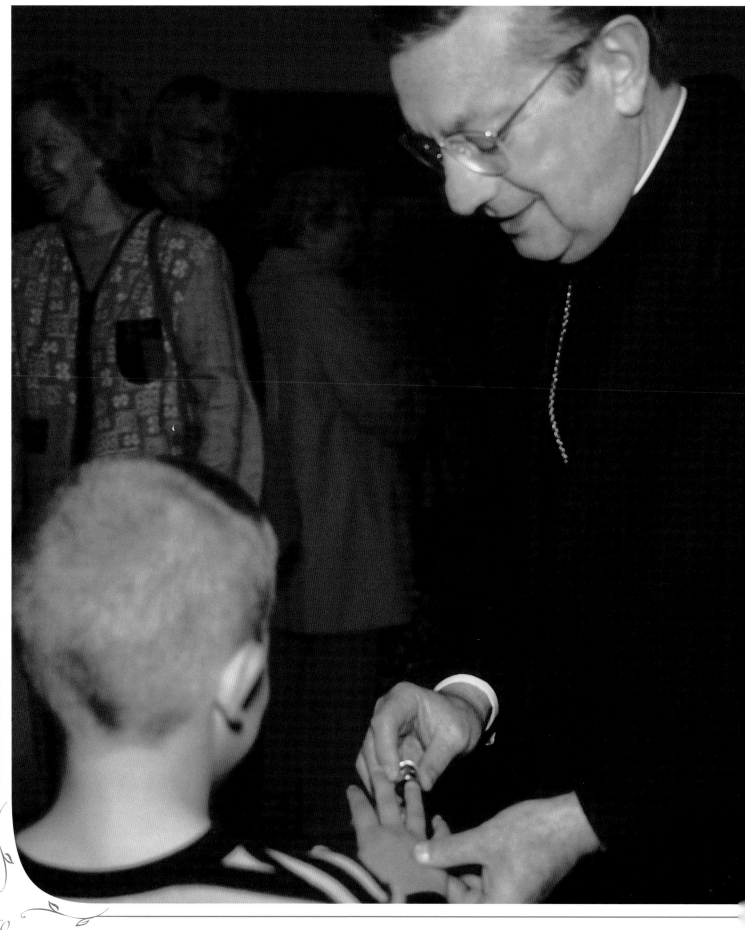

"I challenge you today to unleash the power of your love. I ask you to make it real for me, for your parents, for the people you live and work with, and for your brothers and sisters who desperately need your love. I challenge you today to be fully Christian and to accept the mandate to care for each other. Make Christ alive and real in your world."

"Come Together, We are Church"
Pastoral Letter to Youth and Young Adults
August 26, 1983

*"N*o child is expendable in God's view. All children are precious before our Creator. All must be precious in our eyes. Our children are at risk. Our children are dying. These are the children of all of us. That's why we must create and carry out public policies that treat all God's children as sacred."

Reverend Martin Luther King, Jr. Celebration Homily
January 16, 1992

A sign of his commitment to the Church, the Bishop's Ring is often "tried on for size" by youngsters who show interest in the Bishop's various insignia which, in addition to a ring, include a pectoral cross, a crosier (shepherd's staff), miter (tall hat) and zucchetto (red skull cap).

*"Democracy needs wisdom.
Democracy needs virtue. Democracy
stands or falls with the truths
and values which it embodies and
promotes. Democracy serves what is
true and right when it safeguards
the dignity of every human person,
when it respects inviolable and
inalienable human rights, when it
makes the common good the end and
criterion regulating all public
and social life."*

*City Club Address
January 4, 2002*

*"Our commitment in the Diocese
of Cleveland to ensure the safety
of all our children from the tragedy of
sexual abuse has now reached a
significant point and I am looking to
all of you for your full cooperation
and participation."*

*Letter to the Diocese
Introduction of VIRTUS,
Protecting God's Children Program
June 9, 2003*

For centuries, Catholic members of the legal community have
begun the annual session with a "Red Mass" of the Holy Spirit
asking God's guidance in their deliberations. Bishop Pilla
celebrates annually with local and state justices, judges and
the Catholic Lawyers' Guilds in Cleveland and Akron.

Four priests of the Diocese of Cleveland have been called and ordained as Auxiliary Bishops since 1981: A. Edward Pevec (1982), A. James Quinn (1983), Roger W. Gries, OSB and Martin J. Amos (both in 2001). Pictured is Bishop Martin Amos having just received his Miter (head piece) from Bishop Pilla at his episcopal ordination on June 7, 2001.

*"*Marriage is the basis of the family and families are the foundation of society. The very survival and well-being of all people depends on stable marriages. Marriage is not only for the happiness of two adults, it is a public commitment for the common good of all. This needs to be remembered today.*"*

Statement on Marriage
June 25, 2004

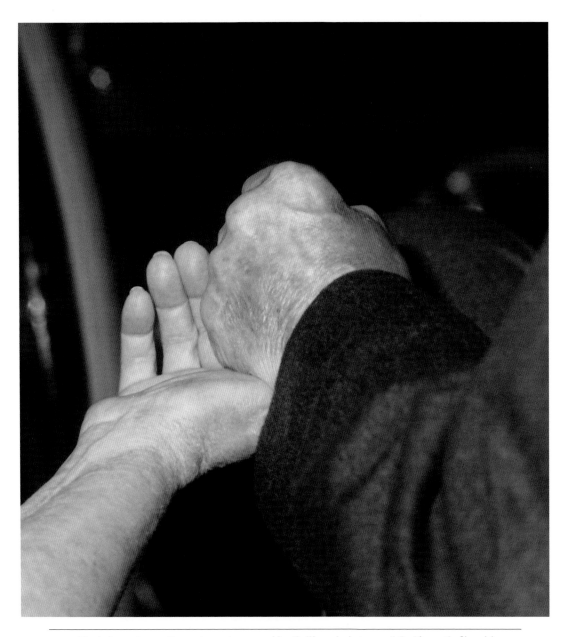

Married couples are the center and source of family life and what we call the 'domestic Church.'
This important role of married people within Church and society is celebrated every July by Bishop Pilla
and over 350 couples at the Golden Wedding Anniversary Mass in the Cathedral of St. John the Evangelist.

"$\mathcal{T}$hose most at risk and most vulnerable have to have a special place in our hearts and minds, in our actions and public policies. Moral convictions must be translated into choices and actions, into policies and practices."

Commission on Catholic Community Action 25th Anniversary
October 29, 1994

The Church in the City Initiative brought the moral perspective to public issues and policies and received national acclaim in the Church and the public sector. Ken Woodward, Newsweek Magazine's Religion Editor, served as moderator of the 1998 Church in the City National Symposium hosted by Bishop Pilla and attended by 1,500 others from around the Diocese and country.

Opposite: National public figures are members of the Body of Christ and members of our local Church. Clevelander and U.S. Senator George Voinovich celebrates the sesquicentennial with the people of the Diocese in August 1997.

"*We must renew our own commitment to live in peace and to work
for peace and justice in our world. Our concern for what happened to our
Holy Father must lead us to commit ourselves to the conversion of our own
lives, to live in faith and hope, to be people of peace. We cannot denounce
the violence that harmed our Holy Father if, in our own lives, violence,
however subtle, is found.*"

Statement on the attempted assassination of our Holy Father
May 14, 1981

Cooperation and prayer with our local public officials is witnessed in this 2003 anniversary of
September 11th. Mayor Jane Campbell has noted that "...when life is painful, where do we want to go but
to this beautiful Cathedral where 'our Bishop' invites us to pray and find consolation and strength."

"You and I will not negotiate a treaty eliminating nuclear weapons. We will not win a Nobel Peace Prize, but we can all do something for peace. We can all be peacemakers. We can all respond compassionately in some way to the plight of our needy sisters and brothers. Each of us can be a glimmer of hope."

Christmas Message
1987

Former Bishop of Cleveland, James Cardinal Hickey of Washington, D.C., represented the Holy See as a Papal Legate for the celebration of the 150th Anniversary of the Diocese in 1997. Bishop Pilla served as Bishop Hickey's Secretary for Clergy and Religious and was ordained by him as Auxiliary Bishop on August 1, 1979.

justice

The Voice of Courage.

"... the moral measure of any community is how the weakest are treated."

Grounded in our community, supported by our faith and commanded by our sense of responsibility, we stand up – particularly for those who have been brought low. Our love of God is translated into a preferential option for the poor. We witness to the sacredness of all life. And we practice the justice of the Bible: "right relationships" in life, family, Church, community, workplace and society.

That way of living becomes a cry, a call for justice. It is faith, made flesh. It is a public stand. It is the practice of love. It offers the gift of hope. Motivated by this call, Bishop Pilla has witnessed and worked for justice among all the children of God. In the last 25 years, as a faithful steward of the richly blessed region of Northeastern Ohio, he has led the Diocese in calling for – and creating – cities and neighborhoods where all God's people can live in a land that truly values community, interdependence and collaboration. This is our kind of justice. This is our faith at work.

The Church has grown to reflect the Bishop's concern for justice for all people. Our many partnerships and collaborations not only accomplish good works, they draw us into loving and just relationships with one another. As defenders of the dignity of every human life, we add our voices and our votes to the national dialogue about which values and visions ought to shape public policy, foreign policy and the laws governing our common good.

By his example, the Bishop has said and shown that these choices are not just economic and political, they are moral and ethical. They determine who will be helped and who will be hurt and how we will move toward the future. Seeking justice makes us a stronger, better, holier people. It is our very nature to be just.

Junior High students engage in dialogue with Bishop Pilla at the "Gandhi-King-Day Event" focusing upon the call to social justice and racial reconciliation inspired by Mahatma Gandhi, Martin Luther King, Jr. and Dorothy Day at Cleveland State University in 1997.

"The Church will uphold the rights of all persons, but especially of those whose rights have been most trampled upon. She will be an advocate for social justice, affirming the human dignity of the poor and loudly condemning the political philosophies, economic policies and social structures that keep people from developing their full potential as human beings."

"A Call to Care for One Another"
Pastoral Letter
October 4, 1981

Bishop Pilla spends time at St. Augustine Hunger Center in Cleveland at the opening celebration of The Libera Pilla Hunger Fund which was established in honor of the Bishop's mother with the goal of endowing the 40 hunger centers and meal programs throughout our eight-county Diocese.

"Let us recommit ourselves to working for the 'beloved community' which Dr. King envisioned and for which he gave his life; a 'beloved community' where racism has no place, where violence is ended and where poverty is unacceptable. Out of his strong religious faith he knew that the journey is long, the road is hard and the struggle for social justice is exacting."

Ecumenical Service,
Lakewood Ministerial Association
Martin Luther King, Jr. Day
January 16, 2000

"I have seen for myself the staggering human cost of violence and poverty in El Salvador. So I am especially grateful for the Central American Peace Plan which offers the first real hope of peace for our long-suffering neighbors in nearly a decade. What a welcome, much needed glimmer of hope."

Christmas Message
December 25, 1987

In the Great Jubilee Year 2000, all bishops were encouraged to take the Good News to those in prison and to form ministries to the incarcerated. Bishop Pilla visited jails in Summit, Medina, Lorain and Cuyahoga counties and initiated on-going ministries in each. He is pictured here enjoying a choir's song prior to Mass in the Cuyahoga County Jail.

"*We must all work together to ensure the physical, social and spiritual renewal of our nation. If we are diligent, our efforts will help repair the social fabric of our families, our communities and our society.*"

National Symposium on The Church in the City Keynote Address
The Temple-Tifereth Israel
April 20, 1998

"*Work is a human right. Every person created in the sacred image of God has the right to dignity and the right to meaningful work. Dignity is realized by participation in community. So every human being has the right to participate fully in the economic and social life of the community through a job.*"

Labor Day Statement
1988

On April 20, 1998, the National Symposium on The Church in the City gathered participants from all denominations, religions and the civic community together for a celebration and dialogue on many challenging social issues at The Temple-Tifereth Israel in Cleveland. It included a live video-link with U.S. Secretary for Housing and Urban Development, Mr. Andrew Cuomo.

*"$\mathcal{T}$he poor are not merely abstractions or statistics. They are
real people and families, single mothers with children, the elderly, new
immigrants. They are members of our churches, mosques and synagogues;
sisters and brothers to us all."*

Interfaith Leaders Addressing Poverty and Welfare Reform in Northeast Ohio
Statement of Collaboration by Catholic, Jewish, Muslim and Protestant Leaders
November 11, 1998

Bishop Pilla joins other Cleveland public officials for the annual Turkey Carving to kick off the Catholic
Charities Thanksgiving meal ministry which is part of the Catholic Hunger and Shelter Network that serves
more than 3.5 million meals each year to hungry people in Northeast Ohio.

"Our lives matter a great deal, not only relative to environmental improvement, but also relative to the building up of God's new creation."

"Christian Faith and the Environment: Reverence and Responsibility"

Feast of St. Francis of Assisi

October 4, 1990

(First Statement on the Environment by a Bishop in the United States)

The Church in the City Initiative draws the rural and the urban together in a mutual concern for farmland preservation and out-migration impact. Bishop Pilla spent a day on this Wayne County dairy farm in 2000.

"Think for a moment about the joy and hopefulness we feel when we see a newborn baby. What a miracle that child is to behold. Too many children do not get the chance to bring that joy. Their lives are ended through abortion. We must work and pray to put an end to abortion."

Respect Life Message
1993

"Your coming together today as leaders in your Catholic high school to share your experiences, hopes and dreams for a more just and peaceful world is a sign of real hope for the Church. I am particularly pleased that you are taking the time to learn more about Catholic Social Teaching...it is an invaluable guide for conscience formation...a 'trustworthy compass' for believers sincerely seeking to follow Jesus more closely."

Letter to Catholic Students for Peace and Justice
August 22, 2004

The preciousness of every life is fundamental to our lives as Catholics and is promoted in this festive way at a youth and young adult ministry event in 2004.

"Through labor, human beings express themselves, actualize themselves. Human labor, therefore, is ennobling because it contributes to the dignity of the human person and to the fulfillment of God's plan for creation."

Letter on Meaningful Work for Every Person
March 2, 1982

"During this holy season of Christmas we are particularly mindful that the Son of God came into the world as a poor child born to a homeless family. We are prepared to join with city, civic and other religious leaders at a table where broader, more systematic issues of homelessness and poverty can be addressed."

Joint Statement of Ecumenical Bishops
Bishop Anthony M. Pilla, Bishop J. Clark Grew, II, Episcopal Diocese of Ohio
and Bishop Marcus J. Miller, Northeastern Ohio Synod,
Evangelical Lutheran Church of America (ELCA)
2001

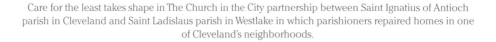

Care for the least takes shape in The Church in the City partnership between Saint Ignatius of Antioch parish in Cleveland and Saint Ladislaus parish in Westlake in which parishioners repaired homes in one of Cleveland's neighborhoods.

*"I'm told The Church in the City is a
real sign of hope. It shows what very
diverse persons and communities can
do together cooperatively for the
common good when they are convened
around a vision that invites them to
reach out, to go beyond where they
are and creatively build on the
best of our shared values."*

*National Pastoral Life Center's
Annual Parish Convention
Sheraton City Center Hotel, Cleveland, Ohio
November 20, 2004*

Ground is broken in Cleveland's Hough/Central
Neighborhood in 1999 for the Fatima Family Center which
is a collaboration among the public sector and the Church
providing some of the most important work we do for justice
through educational, spiritual, recreational and social
programming for all residents of the area.

compassion
Sharing Pain. Sharing Joy.

"It is never too late, God is always there."

While Justice is relentless striving, Compassion grants us the leavening of Grace. Compassion calls forth empathy, forgiveness and the capacity to share in the suffering of all who suffer. As pilgrims on a journey, we become companions of one another when we choose to live with compassion. It carries us back to community in an essential relationship that goes even deeper than solidarity. To truly be with another when he suffers is the richest companionship of all.

Throughout our pilgrimage of hope, we have inevitably stumbled upon many dark moments of pain. With the Bishop's encouragement, we have not fallen. Through his compassion, we have been lifted up. In the grief and pain of life he has spoken words of healing – to the shocked public in the wake of September 11th, to an anxious Church at the death of the Pope, to those mourning their martyred sisters in El Salvador, to parishioners whose church was burned by murderous arson. He has spoken words of apology to victims of sexual abuse. He has spoken frequently to comfort parishes who have lost a beloved pastor. His words have offered solace to the widow of a policeman and to the bereaved mother of a serviceman killed in the line of duty.

In these moments and so many more, we have learned that compassion is key to embracing the death and resurrection of Jesus Himself. When we allow our brothers and sisters to shoulder life's difficulties with us, when we pick up one who is bent with grief – unbearable suffering is transformed into redemption. New life. New love. New hope. It is the mystery of the cross.

The Church of the Diocese of Cleveland under the leadership of Bishop Pilla has formed a communion of compassionate hearts. When life hurts us – even when we have brought it upon ourselves – we have come to expect and be grateful for the tender, steady, simple embrace of the Bishop's compassion. Over these years, the Church has grown to be a company of loving companions – following the shepherd's lead.

The community of believers in the Diocese of Cleveland is a tapestry of nationalities, ages, economic means, races and abilities. Compassion and community call us to be one people embracing one another, providing everyone with access to ministry, fellowship and the love of God.

"When you are seriously ill, you reflect on facing death, and then when you recuperate you reflect on the meaning of your life. You reassess the priorities that you had for yourself up to this time, the way you spent your time and energy. Now every day is a gift."

Reflection on his illness
1997

The elderly and especially those who are infirmed claim a special place within the care of the Church of the Diocese of Cleveland; they are served by 16 church-related and sponsored assisted and long-term living and nursing facilities. Bishop Pilla blesses a member of the community at an outdoor procession.

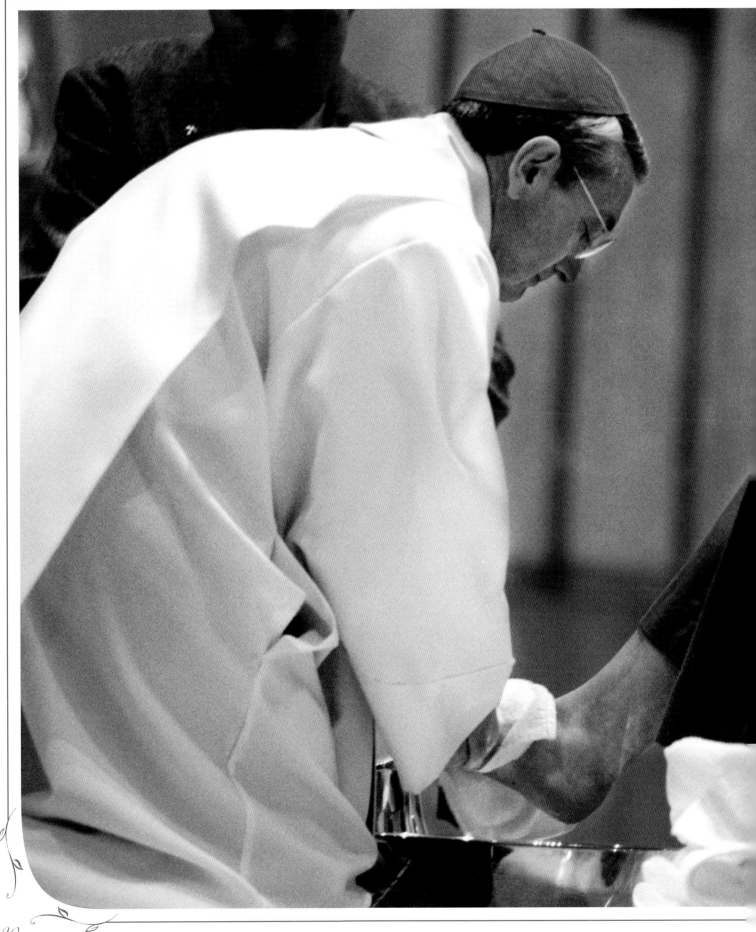

"For the victims of abuse and their parents and families, for all of you good people, for all of you good priests... for all of us, there is a great deal of crucifixion in this painful reality."

Holy Thursday Homily
Cathedral of Saint John the Evangelist
March 29, 2002

The sexual abuse crisis brought the Church to a heightened awareness of the need to protect children and a call to reach out with compassion to victims. As a gesture of reconciliation and healing, Bishop Pilla washed the foot of a victim of clergy sexual abuse on Holy Thursday Mass of the Lord's Supper in 2002 at the Cathedral of St. John the Evangelist.

"We dare not ever forget. Our dear sisters and daughters, Dorothy Kazel and Jean Donovan, are not heroines from our past. Their blood now flows into the redemptive current of the blood of Christ. They are our martyrs, they are our witnesses. Their living examples shall always abide with us."

Installation Mass Homily
Cathedral of Saint John the Evangelist
January 6, 1981

"At the root of violence of all kinds is the escalating disrespect for the sacredness of every human life. Our nation, professing the rights of 'life, liberty and the pursuit of happiness,' seems to grow more and more numb to human loss, human suffering and human indignity."

Statement on Gun-related Violent Deaths
June 1991

Just after being named as Diocesan Bishop, but before his installation, Bishop Pilla had the painful responsibility of presiding at the December 10, 1980, Funeral Mass for Ursuline Sister Dorothy Kazel, OSU, at our Cathedral. Sr. Dorothy was a member of the diocesan mission team in El Salvador who was, together with Cleveland lay-woman Jean Donovan, and Maryknoll Sisters Ita Ford and Maura Clark, martyred by soldiers in El Salvador on December 2, 1980.

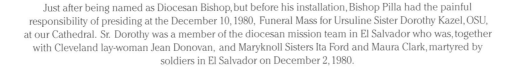

"*We must reach out even more vigorously to people of all ages, races and classes who are experiencing loneliness, rejection or trauma. We need to be visible networks of welcoming and belonging.*"

Easter Message
1990

The physically, mentally and developmentally disabled are some of our Church's most vibrant and valued members. Our Diocesan Ministry to Persons with Disabilities celebrates with the disabled and their families at an annual 'Pilgrimage Mass' and provides all people with access to the faith, education and social services, and encourages their ministries within the Church.

The Diocese mourned the death of Pope John Paul II with a Mass at the Cathedral of St. John the Evangelist on April 5, 2005. Through the Bishop's required visits to Rome every five years and his frequent interactions with the Pope as President of the USCCB, a collaboration and affection developed between the two spiritual leaders.

*"As we struggle in disbelief with the horrifying nature of the incidents at St. Stanislaus,
we look to God to bring us peace and understanding. We also ask for everyone's prayers in order to
bring healing to the families of the victim and the accused, to the Franciscans, to the parish of
St. Stanislaus, to the Slavic Village community and to our Church."*

Statement upon the murder of Franciscan Father William Gulas, OFM
December 9, 2002

In December 2002, the whole Diocese joined the largely Polish-American Saint Stanislaus parish in Cleveland's Slavic Village in shock
and sadness at the murder of their pastor, Fr. William Gulas, OFM, and the arson fire that destroyed the parish rectory. The Bishop joined
in vigil and prayer with the parishioners.

On June 30, 2000, the funeral for slain Cleveland Policeman Wayne Leon was celebrated at the Cathedral of St. John the Evangelist, at which Bishop Pilla presided, a boyhood friend of Officer Leon preached, and safety forces personnel from throughout the country and public officials from our entire region came to pay their respects.

"I was sure of a lot of things when I was ordained. I had a lot of answers. After 38 years of priesthood I know a lot less than I did when I was first ordained because life has taught me that things are very complex. We have to be slow to judge."

Interview on WEWS Television
1995

"To be a loving people, we must first become a compassionate people. Christ not only loved the poor, he understood them and lovingly accepted them."

150th Anniversary of the St. Vincent de Paul Society
1983

"We must work to prove principle by our deeds. Are our beliefs manifested by our behavior? We should be the leaven, the light. The Church must be the voice of the voiceless. A lot of people don't want to hear this."

Interview on his 20th Anniversary
Universe Bulletin Publication
December 22, 2000

While most people were evacuating downtown Cleveland after the 9/11 terrorist attacks upon New York, Washington and Pennsylvania, Bishop Pilla presided at a crowded mid-day Mass at the Cathedral of St. John the Evangelist encouraging our grieving community to be steadfast in the love of God, at peace with our brothers and sisters, and to have compassion even for our attackers. In 2003, a 9/11 Safety Forces Memorial Flagpole was dedicated on the lawn of the Cathedral.

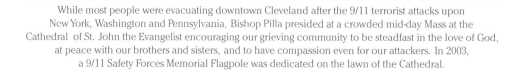

hope

The Promise Fulfilled.

"Because of you, I am full of hope."

Pilgrims who journey with hope as their companion are not easily waylaid by disappointment. In fact, the natural habitat of hope is the darkness of the journey, where shadows darken our understanding and threaten to dislodge us from the path we have undertaken. Without the blindness of our insecurities, hardships and fears, hope would have no place, no role, no purpose.

Like Faith, Responsibility, Justice and Compassion in the Church of the Diocese of Cleveland, Hope takes concrete form in the face of life's difficulties. We have a saying, "Your love is their hope." In the presence of poverty, abuse, neglect, discouragement and obstacles of every kind, the care and ministry of the Church offers real hope.

In this quarter of a century, Bishop Pilla has led our Catholic Charities ministries to become the largest in the world – serving over 600,000 clients each year: the disabled, the elderly, the homeless, the hungry, the young, the addicted, the unborn and so many others who need and deserve our care. They long for hope.

Hope is the virtue that turns our eyes to the future. The Bishop has always emphasized the role that young people have in the Church of today

– it is they to whom the future belongs. The gift of life and faith are the entitlement of our children, but in the mission of our Church, their education is our driving concern. There is little hope for children without a quality education. So many, especially the children of our urban centers, languish without the hope that a good education can offer. Bishop Pilla's leadership has focused upon the maintenance and development of schools and ministries where these children are loved, nurtured and taught. This is the richness of hope; this is the uniqueness of our local Church. By sharing love today, we touch and transform the future.

Being Catholic is a calling that we embrace and a yoke of service that is laid upon the pilgrims who walk the way of Christ. The Bishop has reminded us that our inheritance, and our legacy, is to "care for the least." That is what Jesus would do, and that is what Jesus continues to do through us. Indeed, when those in need ask "who is my neighbor?", the Church of the Diocese of Cleveland has answered with lavish care and generous love. We are their neighbors. We offer them hope.

Hope shines as a light in the darkness. This youngster participates in a 2002 evening vigil in the wake of death and devastation at Saint Stanislaus parish rectory in Slavic Village.

"*In the midst of sin, evil materialism and our own weakness, Christ confirms us as bearers of hope and reconciliation for a broken world. We are not held back by the darkness of what, through sin, we have been. We are moving forward, led by the light of what, through redemption, we are yet to be.*"

Installation Mass Homily
Cathedral of Saint John the Evangelist
January 6, 1981

Prayer is the heart of the Church's life and it is the birthplace of hope. Bishop Pilla leads the community in a prayer for light and hope.

"There is a goodness and a giftedness in each of you that must be acknowledged and nurtured and affirmed. You bring to this world of ours, this Church of ours, a perspective that can cause us to see our faith with a different vision. You hold exciting visions of what tomorrow could be. Your idealism is a sign of hope."

Come Together, We are Church
Pastoral Letter to Youth and Young Adults
August 26, 1983

We all face various challenges. The physically and mentally disabled are fully incorporated members of our Church's life and ministries. This father and son enjoy a day at a recent diocesan family event.

Opposite: Residents and friends of Jennings Center for Older Adults in Garfield Heights, Ohio, gather as Bishop Pilla blesses a prayer garden. Jennings is one of over 25 such Catholic facilities offering independent, assisted, skilled nursing, Alzheimer, hospice, Adult Day Care and many other forms of care.

"This evening we come together not to mourn but to celebrate, to renew in ourselves the belief that goodness shall overcome evil, that life is stronger than death, that the kingdom of God shall come. As Archbishop Romero asked with the last words he spoke, 'Let us be united in faith and hope.'

Ecumenical/Interrelgious Memorial Service for Archbishop Romero
March 24, 1981

The Light of Christ surrounds us and gives us a glimmer of hope. Among others joining Bishop Pilla
in a 1997 candlelight prayer in the Cathedral of St. John the Evangelist are Archbishop Daniel Pilarczyk,
the Archbishop of Cincinnati (what is known as the Metropolitan of the Six Dioceses in the State of Ohio) and
Cleveland Auxiliary Bishop A. James Quinn.

"Ɠod's promise to all of us, and God's calling for us as individuals and as a Church, in a word, is 'home.' Like the prophet Isaiah, my mom knew what the essential quality of a home was; the essence of home is 'to be cherished and never forgotten'."

Funeral Mass Homily for Bishop Pilla's Mother, Libera Pilla
Cathedral of Saint John the Evangelist
February 1, 2003

Feeding the hungry is the command of Christ and in doing so we have grown in the likeness of Jesus Himself. Bishop Pilla visits here in one of 76 hunger centers and ministries operated by various agencies and non-profit organizations with the support of our Diocesan Catholic Charities.

*"An important part of a Catholic school's mission
is to offer students from all socioeconomic, racial and ethnic
backgrounds a community that cares and challenges, and
an education that empowers and liberates."*

Leadership Cleveland
March 16, 1988

Nearly 60,000 youngsters attend over 150 parochial, diocesan and independent Catholic schools from Pre-Kindergarten to the 12th Grade. Likewise, three Catholic colleges within the Diocese offer undergraduate and graduate degrees. Education is a sign and an instrument of hope.

Opposite: The next generation and the new immigrants are a sign of our hope for the future. Through our Parish Life Secretariat the growing number of new immigrants are welcomed into church life and community. This young girl in traditional Korean dress participates in the annual Asian Ministry Mass with an offering of flowers.

*"So continue the good that you are doing and continue to
share the good news with others. We need to hear that good news.
We need to know about these signs of hope in our city. And take
comfort in the realization that God knows all the good you are doing.
That's what really matters."*

Dedication Remarks
Project Afford Housing
2000

The semi-annual Alleluia Ball engages corporate and private donors to support the tuition assistance program of the Diocese and in 2004 the
proceeds hit an all-time high of $1 million. Bishop Pilla greets 2004 Alleluia Ball Chairperson Maria Miller and her husband, Sam Miller.

The source of hope for so many of the children in our needy neighborhoods is a solid Catholic education. The tuition assistance program in 2004 alone distributed $1.8 million to deserving and promising young people. Pictured here are choir members from Saint Louis parish elementary school in Cleveland Heights who performed at the 2004 Alleluia Ball.

"We often hear that alcoholism and drug dependency are the most serious public health problems in the United States today. I am very concerned about this, especially as it affects the people of this Diocese. I know it is a problem that affects not only the user, but one that touches the lives of so many families in our parishes."

"Faith and Freedom from Addiction"
Pastoral Letter
March 24, 1991

"You have been blessed and gifted. I urge you to consider seriously how you can share those blessings and gifts with others, especially with those who have not been so fortunate. Our world cries out today for persons of maturity and generosity willing to apply their talents for the betterment of society."

Commencement Address
Cleveland State University
June 6, 1991

Participants in the Easter Vigil raise their candles as a sign of the light of Christ overcoming the darkness. Several members of the diocesan staff participated with others in a nationally televised Easter Special from the Cathedral of St. John the Evangelist in the spring of 1997.

Opposite: The hope-filled finale of the 'Fest' each year is a candlelit Eucharistic celebration with a choir of over 200 members, big screen display, fireworks and an estimated 14,000 participants.

"$\mathcal{T}$he idealism that is in you, that drives you each day to make this a better world, I think, is the Spirit moving. God wants us to make this a better world. God wants us to be a compassionate, hope-filled people."

Greater Cleveland YMCA Annual Meeting
1998

Youth and Young Adult Ministry is vital to the Diocese of Cleveland and our youth are supported by many diocesan, parish and campus ministries including "Life Teen" that has impacted so many young people in the last decade. Thousands of youth enjoy Christian Rock music and fun activities annually at the 'Fest.'

Opposite: The annual Catholic Charities appeal has raised hundreds of millions of dollars for direct care of the poor and social service ministries in all eight counties of the Diocese. Many of the beneficiaries of this work of the Church are children and young people as pictured here with Bishop Pilla in 1995.

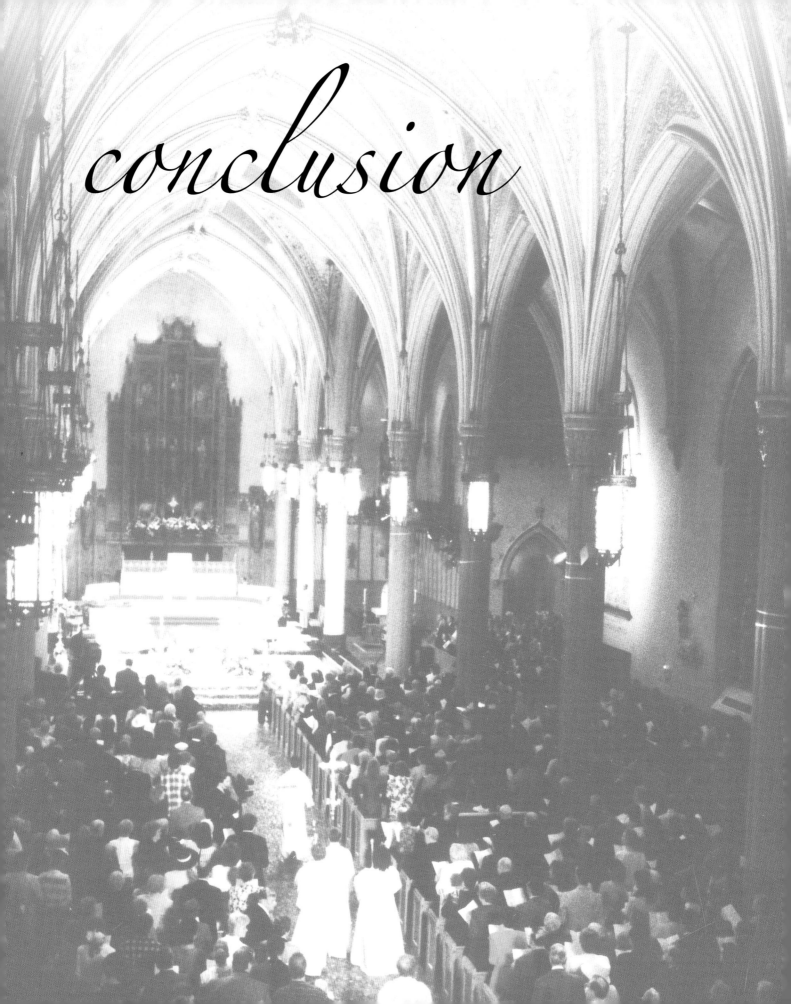

conclusion

"Live on in my love."

A pilgrimage begun and continued in the spirit and promise of hope is eternal – rich and complete in each moment. When a long span of time has elapsed and many miles have been traveled, hope reveals that, even then, what appears to be an ending is in fact a renewal, a rebirth. Hope, like faith and love, endures forever.

This steadfastness of spirit is surely the heritage and the promise of the Church of the Diocese of Cleveland. We have paused here, at what might appear to be an end of our 25-year pilgrimage, to celebrate and remember, to honor and recommit, even to mourn and rejoice with our brother and Bishop, Anthony. But the eyes of faith can see that this place is not our destination. This moment holds the same hope that we were called to embrace when we began.

The community of friends that has grown up around the life, ministry, teaching and witness of Bishop Anthony M. Pilla believes and teaches that each generation in every age has a privilege and a responsibility to bear the light of hope to the world. As our ancestors so ably and humbly did before us, so it has been given us to do. What they have done with so little we are called to do with what appears to be so much.

When we have walked this path of hope faithfully, our boast will be nothing more than that "we have done our part – we have borne the light of hope for another leg of the journey." The most important judgment of us will be the measure to which our descendants follow where we have trod – to be bearers of the light of hope.

This Jubilee, like every celebration of life on our journey, can be an occasion of true jubilation if we will move on from this place of reflection and step back onto our chosen path together, refreshed and exultant, uplifted, bearing the light of Christ in the world. In that way, we are truly Pilgrims of Hope!

afterword

My Dear Brothers and Sisters in Christ,

As an "afterword" for this book, I want to share some of my personal thoughts and convictions.

I wish first to tell you of God's great goodness to me. When I did not know which way to turn, He gave me direction. When I did not measure up to His expectations, He forgave me over and over again. He has given me strength and motivation needed to continue the struggle. He has always been present to wipe away the tears of discouragement and loneliness. So often all I could produce were the proverbial crooked lines. Yet somehow, He always managed to write straight with them.

Mary, the Blessed Mother, has also played an important role in my life. She has been a model and source of inspiration and strength for me. Her greatness rests in her intense faith, which prompted her to accept God's will joyfully and without hesitation. Her example and intercession have been a precious gift to me.

What have been the happiest times of my ministry? I can answer without hesitation: the times when I have been nearest to the people – when I could bring them the beauty and richness of Christ's Word and the consolation and the healing power of His sacraments; when I could share their joys and sorrows; when I could give them assurance that – notwithstanding all our shortcomings and failures – we are all important in the Lord's eyes.

Contemporary society has its own standards for judging a person's success. But nothing of what the world calls success can begin to compare with the grace-filled experiences I have had in ministering to people. The satisfaction that comes from such ministry is the greatest reward. It is far better than prominence, official position, or the fleeting applause of crowds.

One final word. The Church of today is quite different from the Church of twenty-five years ago. It has not always been easy to adapt. There have been times when I was perplexed and troubled. It is my hope that the turmoil of these years has been the birth pangs of a new age and a renewed Church. Far from weakening my faith, the events of these years have strengthened it. My union with the Lord has become more intimate and decisive.

For all of this I express my gratitude to God and to you, the good people of the Diocese of Cleveland, who have supported and encouraged me. May the Lord bless us as, together, we rededicate ourselves to Him and each other.

Sincerely yours in Christ,

acknowledgments

A project of this magnitude can only happen with the collaboration, support, and dedication of talented, faithful and generous contributors. The quality, the artistry and the substance of this book reflect the genuine goodness of its subject – the people of the Diocese of Cleveland and episcopacy of Bishop Anthony M. Pilla. The beauty of this edition is evidence of the skill and the gifts of those who conceived, developed and produced it, in particular, the staff of Liggett-Stashower under the generous direction of Evelyn Allen, the writing of Ann Hogsett and the artwork and book design of Petra Dunlap.

The sponsors of this book have, through their generosity, enabled us to produce and distribute this dignified, first-quality historic photo-archive with all of the proceeds going to the establishment of the Bishop Pilla Legacy of Hope Jubilee Foundation. We are so grateful to: Ann and David Brennan; Mr. Vincent Campanella; Carfagna Family Foundation; Maryellen and Umberto Fideli and Family; The Goudreau Family in memory of George J. and Lenore A. Goudreau, Sr.; Mr. and Mrs. Kenneth A. Lanci; Mrs. Norma Lerner in memory of Alfred Lerner; Mr. and Mrs. Patrick F. McCartan; Samuel H. and Maria Miller Foundation in appreciation to Bishop Pilla for doing more over the last 25 years than any other U.S. prelate to bring the Catholic and Jewish communities together; Mr. and Mrs. Murlan J. Murphy, Sr. and Family; William J. and Katherine T. O'Neill; Mr. Nacy Panzica; The Pilla Family; Peter and Celeste Spitalieri in the name of the PAS Foundation.

Their support is recognition of Bishop Pilla's impact upon our Church and all the people of our metropolitan area and many years of friendship, collaboration and admiration.

The Project Committee worked very hard to get the story right so that the image of the Church and the record of this period of history were presented thoroughly and respectfully. With gratitude we mention them and the offices they represent: Sr. Rita Mary Harwood, SND, Secretariat for Parish Life and Development; Mr. Robert Tayek, Diocesan Communications Office; Mr. Leonard Calabrese and Sr. Kathleen Ryan, SND, both of the Catholic Commission on Community Action; Miss Christine Krosel, Diocesan Archives; Mr. Edward Mayer, Catholic Diocese of Cleveland Foundation; Mr. Joseph Polito, the Catholic Universe Bulletin; and the co-chairpersons for this project, Sr. Laura Bouhall, OSU, Chancery Office; and Reverend Edward T. Estok, Jr., Administrative Assistant to Bishop Pilla.

Photography attribution:

Anthony Cannata, title page, p. 16, p. 21; Catholic News Service, Nancy Wiechec, p. 32; Catholic News Service, Nancy Wiechec, p. 58; Felici Fotografia, Rome, p. 42; The Cleveland Plain Dealer, David I. Anderson, p. 74; The Cleveland Plain Dealer, Eustacio Humphrey, p. 90; The Cleveland Plain Dealer, Marvin Fong, p. 95; The Cleveland Plain Dealer, Chuck Crowe, p. 97; The Akron Beacon Journal, Greg Ruffing, p. 96 and p. 102; and pictures contributed by Joseph Darwal, Jack Forestal, Pat Hendrick, Maribeth Joeright, Michael Knaus, Philip Leiter, Tony Morrison, Joan Nemeth, Peter Nguyen, Thomas Ondrey, Steven Otlowski, William Rieter, Dennis Sadowski, Stephanie Saniga, George Shuba, MG Studios, Inc., other photographers of The Catholic Universe Bulletin, and many parishioners, religious and members of the Catholic Diocese of Cleveland.